Sophokles Antigone

Sophokles

translated by Anne Carson

With an introduction by Laura Jansen

methuen | drama
LONDON • NEW YORK • OXFORD • NEW DELHI • SYDNEY

METHUEN DRAMA
Bloomsbury Publishing Plc, 50 Bedford Square, London, WC1B 3DP, UK
Bloomsbury Publishing Inc, 1359 Broadway, New York, NY 10018, USA
Bloomsbury Publishing Ireland, 29 Earlsfort Terrace, Dublin 2, D02 AY28, Ireland

BLOOMSBURY, METHUEN DRAMA and the Methuen Drama logo are trademarks of Bloomsbury Publishing Plc

First published in Great Britain by Oberon Books 2015

This edition published by Methuen Drama in the Modern Classics series 2026

Cover design: Ben Anslow

A catalogue record for this book is available from the British Library.

A catalog record for this book is available from the Library of Congress.

ISBN: PB: 978-1-3506-0037-9
ePDF: 978-1-3506-0038-6
eBook: 978-1-3506-0039-3

Series: Modern Classics

Typeset by Newgen KnowledgeWorks Pvt. Ltd., Chennai, India
Printed and bound in Great Britain

For product safety related questions contact productsafety@bloomsbury.com.

To find out more about our authors and books visit www.bloomsbury.com and sign up for our newsletters.

Contents

Introduction, by Laura Jansen vii

A Note from The Translator xvi

Sophokles. Antigone, translated by Anne Carson 1

Methuen Drama Modern Classics

Methuen Drama's *Modern Classics* series showcases landmark plays from around the world. Drawing on the *Modern Plays* series, which launched in 1959, *Modern Classics* celebrates plays from the contemporary repertoire by world-leading dramatists and presents their work in a definitive edition, alongside new introductions by leading scholars and industry professionals. With writers such as Pulitzer Prize-winners Jackie Sibblies Drury, Ayad Akhtar and David Mamet through to Lucy Prebble, Katori Hall and Caryl Churchill, *Modern Classics* are ideal for students and anyone wanting to deepen their knowledge of the plays that form part of the modern dramatic canon.

Sophokles Antigone

A marvellous new translation by Anne Carson that crackles with canny colloquialism and insight – Arts Desk

When her dead brother is decreed a traitor, Antigone refuses to leave his body unburied. Defying her uncle's governance she forges ahead with the funeral alone, placing personal allegiance before politics, a tenacious act that will trigger a cycle of destruction.

T.S. Eliot Prize-winning poet Anne Carson, offers a vivid translation of Sophokles' tragic masterpiece that was first staged in a ground-breaking production at the Barbican in 2015, directed by Ivo van Hove.

A raw and beautiful adaption, *Sophokles. Antigone* is published in Methuen Drama's Modern Classics series, featuring a new introduction by Laura Jansen.

Anne Carson is a MacArthur Fellow; she has received the Lannan Prize, the T.S. Eliot Prize, the Pushcart Prize, the Griffin Poetry Prize (twice-awarded), and was an Anna-Maria Kellen Fellow at the American Academy in Berlin, Germany. Anne adapted *The Bakkhai* for the Almeida in 2015. Classic Stage Company in New York has produced *An Oresteia* (a trilogy adapted from Aeschylus' *Agamemnon*, Sophokles' *Electra* and Euripides' *Orestes*) in repertory. *Norma Jeanne Baker of Troy* (a version of Euripides' *Helen*) has been staged at The Shed in New York. An opera-version of *H of H Playbook* will be produced in Basel in 2027, composed by Bruce Dessner.

Introduction

unusual girl that she is
(Anne Carson, 'A Note from The Translator', *Sophokles. Antigone*. 2015: 5)

I'm a strange new kind of inbetween thing aren't I
(*Sophokles. Antigone*, Translated by Anne Carson. 2015: 39)

You may be approaching these pages with knowledge of Belgian theatre director Ivo van Hove's stage production 'Antigone'. This play toured with great success (and some criticism, too) in Luxembourg, London, Edinburgh, and parts of the USA in 2015. With famous French actress Juliette Binoche in the leading role, it has arguably become an instantly recognisable stage performance of Sophocles' tragedy in English. But have you read *Sophokles. Antigone*, the 'translation-play' that Canadian poet, classical scholar, translator, and visual artist Anne Carson (1950–) produced for van Hove's staged play and which follows this introduction? If you haven't yet, you will discover that there's nothing quite like it!

First things first, though, in case you haven't yet read Sophocles' tragedy. Produced around 442–441 BCE, his *Antigone* was performed at the Festival of Dionysus in Athens that year, earning the tragedian the first prize. In Sophocles' version (for he was not the only ancient Greek tragedian to retell Antigone's tragic myth; his near contemporary Euripides had his own version, now lost), the story goes something like this. Four siblings – Polynices, Eteocles, Ismene, and Antigone – are the offspring of King Oedipus of Thebes and his wife Jocasta, whose brother is the formidable Creon, Antigone's uncle. Following Oedipus' death, Polynices and Eteocles take turns to rule Thebes; yet this arrangement does not work out, and a quarrel for power ensues between them, culminating in Eteocles' usurpation of the throne and Polynices' expulsion from Thebes. There follows a bloody battle for political and territorial power between the Theban and Argive armies – led by Eteocles and Polynices, respectively – in which the two brothers are killed. When

Creon becomes king, he declares Polynices a traitor of Thebes, and decrees that he is not to be buried or mourned in customary state and religious fashion. But Antigone boldly defies her uncle's order and somehow manages to bury her beloved brother outside the city walls, even as her sister Ismene warns her repeatedly of the dire consequences of her civil disobedience: namely, of setting the laws of the state against those of the gods. Spoiler alert: Antigone is caught – dramatically so – and this leads to a tragic chain of events, culminating in her suicide by hanging. Yet disaster also awaits other key characters: Creon, his wife Eurydice, and his son Haemon. A tragic drama indeed.

Sophokles. Antigone is not Anne Carson's first rendition of Sophocles' tragedy. Before this translation play, she published an experimental graphic adaptation titled *Antigonick* (2012), winner of the John D. Criticos Prize for 'original work that reflects on ancient Greece'. *Antigonick* is a book composed of aquarelle illustrations by Bianca Stone alongside Carson's own handwriting in black and red ink, the latter colour surely symbolising brotherly blood. Both renderings, *Sophokles. Antigone* and *Antigonick*, speak intimately to Carson's reception of Sophocles and the drama of a sister who loses a brother whom she cannot bury – at least, not in the way she would have hoped. Antigone's experience resonates with Carson's own: her elder brother, Michael, passed away in 2000, a personal tragedy that Carson vividly commemorates in yet another avant garde work – her highly acclaimed *Nox* (2010). This accordion-shaped book, housed in a coffin-like box made out of text, photographs, and sketches, is something of a consolation monument to Michael, who died unexpectedly in Denmark, too far from Carson's home in Canada for her to see him buried. In *Nox*, Carson reworks poem 101 by the Roman author Catullus, which he composed when his own brother died far from home (this time, Asia Minor). *Nox*, *Antigonick*, and *Sophokles. Antigone* form part of a network of works on brother-sister relations, the death of a sibling, their burials, and the various ways of mourning their loss – themes that go back to her sustained reading of Catullus and, above all, Sophocles' *Antigone*.

Elsewhere in Carson's oeuvre, Antigone is implicit in other Sophoclean figures, like Electra: the 'bedless, unwed, unmarriageable' daughter of Agamemnon and Clytemnestra, whose single power is to say 'no'. As Carson puts it in her introduction to her translation of *Elektra*, 'her function [has] been reduced to one activity – saying *no* to everything around her. *No* to her father's murder at the hands of her mother … *no* to her life as if nothing were wrong … *no* to breaking off her lament'. Carson concludes that 'Sophokles is a playwright fascinated … by people who say *no* … people who resist compromise … like Ajax or Antigone' (*An Oresteia*, p. 78).

Translations of Sophocles' play into English abound. Some aim at a degree of fidelity to the ancient Greek, such as Hugh Lloyd Jones' Loeb edition (1994), regularly consulted by students learning Greek at school and university. Other translations have gained wider recognition, such as Robert Fagles' *Penguin Classics* rendition (1984) which, as the back cover tells us, is renowned for conveying 'Sophocles' lucidity and power: the cut and thrust of his dialogue, his ironic edge, the surge and majesty of his choruses and, above all, the agonies and triumphs of his characters'. Then there is Anne Carson's rendering, the one you are holding in your hands, or viewing on your screen. Flick or scroll through it: have you noticed the utter absence of punctuation marks, the hallmark use of Ks instead of Cs to transliterate the Greek kappa (κ) in order to intensify this letter's sound (you can try saying it aloud: Sophokles, Kreon, Bakkhos), the exclamatory 'O's without the h ('O tomb | o bridal chamber | O house in the ground forever', cries Antigone as she buries Polynices, p. 40), the economy of language, often brisk and wittily colloquial ('what's up, Teiresias', says Kreon, in response to the blind seer's solemn address: 'hail, you kings of Thebes', p. 43)? Add to this the heterogenous distribution of words across the page that make your eyes err up and down, left and right, as if you were seeing language perform on the stage (single-word lists, zig-zags, uneven margins, blank spaces in between), together with a series of somewhat puzzling, incomplete utterances, usually ending in 'what' ('KREON: here's Kreon | perfect for what', p. 25; 'CHORUS: here comes Kreon … | dragging his what', p. 51).

'This is not serious; it means nothing at all!' a student of mine uttered with frustration in Greek class. 'Tch-tch, you don't get it, do you? She's dead serious about it all; she knows her Greek, and makes it raw and real for us!' responded another, by now a Carson convert. Such seems to be the constant reception of Carson's approach to translating Sophocles' *Antigone*, Greek tragedy, and the Greco-Roman classics more broadly: readers' responses fluctuate between unreserved admiration and a sense of knowing, on the one hand, and unsettled confusion and shock, on the other. For me, though, the aspects of Carson's writing that provoke such reactions are precisely what makes her translation-play *Antigone* a true 'modern classic': like Sophocles' heroine, it is bold, non-conformist, and utterly radical. This may also be what Juliette Binoche tried to convey in a recorded interview at the Barbican Centre in London, where von Hove's 'Antigone' opened in March 2015. At one point, the actress – who had to take elocution lessons to master the style of Carson's script – reflects on the tenor of this rendition, its hard-to-pin-down quality (note the pauses in her response as she searches for words, which I have marked with ellipses): 'Anne Carson's translation has this power, you know … the power of poetry … but also directness – it's very direct … it's like "skin and bones"… and there is so much space in it … because it feels simple … and yet there is the epic sense of the language … there [are] some moments which are very poetic; this space allows [for] imagination and emotions …' A sound reading indeed, coming from someone who spent an intense period of time memorising, rehearsing, and perfecting the utterance of Carson's lines.

Yet I suspect that there's a bit more to it. Let me take you through a couple of examples that may help to illustrate some of the lexical experiments in this rare translation-play (or contemporary play on a much older play). Take, for instance, the second choral song (p. 23), uttered by the 'Chorus of Old Theban Men' after they hear of Kreon's decree and the Guard's account of the mysterious burial that has taken place outside the city walls. Compare my own deliberately literal translation (right column) of the Greek from Lloyd-Jones' edition (lines 332–33, left column) with Carson's rendering (immediately below):

πολλὰ τὰ δεινὰ κοὐδὲν ἀν-	Many things are terrible, but none
θρώπου δεινότερον πέλει·	come to be more terrible than man!

CHORUS:

many things strange

terrible
clever
wonderous
monstrous
marvellous
dreadful
awful
and
weird
there are in the world
but none more

strange
terrible
clever
uncanny
wondrous
monstrous
marvellous
dreadful
awful
and weird
than Man

The most obvious difference between these three texts is in length, with Carson's rendition featuring 31 words as opposed to 7 in the original Greek and 13 in my literal translation (but I could have used only 9: 'Many things are terrible, but none more than man!'). This is an instance in which the economy of language that characterises most of Carson's translation is completely turned around, or 'catastrophised', as she likes to put it. Our term 'catastrophe' comes from the Greek *katastrophē*, meaning literally an 'overturning' or 'sudden turn'; this is an important term in the study of the tragic plot, broadly used to convey the disastrous, dramatic reversal of fortune that leads to a protagonist's ruin and downfall. Carson uses this concept of catastrophe to combat 'clichés' in her translation process and thought ('Variations on the Right to Remain Silent', *Float* 2016). Such is the case with the above lines of Sophocles' *Antigone.* For Carson, the word 'terrible' alone does not seem quite enough to communicate Sophocles' take on mankind at this crucial point of his play. The word in ancient Greek that I have translated as 'terrible', δεινός (*deinos*), has a wide spectrum of meaning, which the Chorus may well be attempting to articulate as they reflect on the nature of humanity more broadly: humans are 'terrible', 'terrifying', 'dangerous', 'dreadful', 'awful' creatures; but they can also be 'awesome', 'strange', 'wondrous', 'clever', 'adept' – even 'remarkable'. Carson conveys this augmented meaning through two nearly exhaustive 'dictionary' word-lists, placed on separate columns but joined together by the main comparative clause: 'many things strange ... but none more ... than Man' (the similarity between the first and last words of this clause – 'many' and 'Man' – suggest a kind of ring composition). These 'many strange things' cannot be dismissed as simply 'terrible' – not in a tragic drama that uncovers so many other cognate emotions about humans, from wonderment and cleverness to the monstrous and plain weird. In this sense, Carson's 'translation-catastrophe' is paradoxically 'faithful' on her part, for she appeals to a metaphor that echoes the catastrophic structure of tragedy itself.

In my last example, Carson's synthetic economy of words deliberately leaves a question mark, or an unexplained space, towards the end of her translation-play, at a point when everything goes horribly (but also, following Carson, wondrously, monstrously, weirdly!) wrong for Kreon. The king walks towards the centre of the stage holding his son's dead body in his arms – at least, we assume this is what he carries, as Sophocles leaves this a bit unclear. As he does so, the Chorus utters (p. 51):

καὶ μὴν ὅδ' ἄναξ αὐτὸς ἐφήκει	Here comes the king himself,
μνῆμ' ἐπίσημον διὰ χειρὸς ἔχων,	holding in his arms a clear reminder:
εἰ θέμις εἰπεῖν, οὐκ ἀλλοτρίαν	if one may say so, his ruin [comes not] from others,
ἄτην, ἀλλ' αὐτὸς ἁμαρτών.	but from his own mistake.

CHORUS: here comes Kreon
dragging his
dragging his
drawing his what
no one else did this
he did this

You may ask, as my students do, how Carson goes from Sophocles' 'holding in his arms a clear reminder' to 'dragging his what'. One can only guess at the thought process behind Carson's rendering of these lines (and even when one interviews the poet, as I have, her answers still leave you at 'what'!). At first, this appears to be a simple case of poetic repetition ('dragging his | dragging his | dragging his what'), something we find elsewhere in Carson's translation of this play (including the repetition of the word 'what'), but also crucially in Sophocles' original. But let's move beyond this cliché and instead follow Carson's philosophy of translation-as-catastrophe. Sophocles' original text does not explicitly reveal whether Creon is carrying his son's Haemon's body literally or symbolically, or indeed if it is his attendants who do so. The lines may well mean that Creon's hands (the literal meaning of the Greek word I have translated as 'arms' – χείρ, *kheir* – is 'hand') bear 'a clear reminder' of the consequences of his actions, i.e. there is blood on his hands, rather than a body. Add to this the range of meaning of μνῆμ' ἐπίσημον (*mnēm' episēmon*), a phrase in Greek that can be rendered as a 'distinct reminder', 'clear monument', 'imprint memory', or even – if we take 'clearly visible' – 'a speaking remembrance'. Put differently, the range of translation possibilities is multiple, to the point that the word becomes an 'untranslatable' (a concept Carson discusses in 'A Note from The Translator' preceding this introduction). No rendering will quite give us the 'what' in a way that accurately reflects on the drama of Kreon's tragic error. Hence, if I am following the right path here, Carson opts for 'what' as an attempt to convey the uncertain meaning of this tricky line: 'he is dragging, dragging … dragging in his arms, but dragging what?' In doing so, Carson deliberately 'catastrophises' the meaning of Sophocles' original Greek. This 'catastrophic' rendering elegantly replicates the unclarity (for us) of Sophocles' 'clearly visible' reminder – a *mnēma* we can't see because we know his tragedy only through the intermediary of the text. In that sense, Carson's rendering is also a fiercely 'loyal' rendering – overturning Sophocles' clarity in a way that is faithful to the original phrase's lack of clarity – or need for visual completion. Carson's 'what' could be flagging the very fact that we have access only to Sophocles script, not to the performed play.

If I have made this introduction a bit difficult towards the end, this is because Carson is not an easy thinker, and to conceive of her *Sophokles. Antigone* as a modern classic is by no means straightforward. But you may find that this difficulty is what makes her translation-play so compelling, so utterly fascinating. She pushes you to think beyond the obvious – clichés, standardisations, traditional expectations – and then challenges you a bit more, never quite settling on a single meaning, always raising the possibility that someone or something conveys more than it first appears to. So, too, does Sophocles' *Antigone*, whose enduring appeal centres on its remarkable capability to be adapted and reinterpreted afresh each time, whether as an ancient Greek drama handsomely produced on the stages of Luxemburg and London, or as a modestly budgeted play performed underground in Argentina during the military juntas of the last quarter of the twentieth century. Carson's *Sophokles. Antigone* can be putatively adapted to both scenarios; for, 'unusual girl that she is', she occupies 'a strange new kind of inbetween' (Carson's own descriptions of her heroine, cited as the epigraphs to this introduction). But you may just decide to leave my words behind and simply enjoy Carson's 'play on a play' as it is. Let it wash over you. And I suspect Carson would be fine with this, too.

LAURA JANSEN

Fradinger, Moira. 2023. *Antígonas: Writing from Latin America*. Oxford: Oxford University Press.

Griffith, Mark (ed.). 1999. *Sophocles Antigone*. Cambridge: Cambridge University Press.

Jansen, Laura (ed.). 2022. *Anne Carson/Antiquity*. London: Bloomsbury Academic.

Mee, Erin B., and Foley, Helene P. (eds). 2012. *Antigone on the Contemporary World Stage*. Oxford: Oxford University Press.

A Note from The Translator

Let me share with you the problem of untranslatability. Two examples.

At line 943 of this play Antigone utters her final words as a living person and exits to her death. She has just sung her own funeral dirge, unusual girl that she is, and the dirge ends with her summary statement of what she did wrong, the reason why she is condemned to die. Her tone is raw, astounded and sad, yet also unshakable. It makes no sense to her that things worked out the way they did, still she remains clear about the moral quotient of the situation. She expresses all this in a sentence that is almost a paradox:

> I was caught in an act of perfect piety
>
> (943)

Surely piety is not a criminal act in which one is "caught"? Surely piety is a good thing? Surely the community that outlaws an act of perfect piety is a community that has tipped over the edge into nonsense? Antigone stands poised on this edge, holding onto sense.

Her wording emphasizes the precariousness of the moment: it is top-heavy with meaning. She has loaded two cognates of the same word (noun, verb) on top of one another in a way that is standard rhetorical procedure in Greek but sounds overdetermined in English, as if to say:

> I have been completely pious in committing
> an act of complete piety

Both noun (*eusebia*) and verb (*sebizo*) derive from the Greek root *seb-*, which refers to the awe that radiates from gods to humans and is given back as worship. Everything related to this root has fear in it. But *eusebia* is a fear that moves as devotion – a striving out of this world into another and a striving out of another world into this. A kind of permanent elsewhere[1] located "in" human being.

Now consider the English word "piety". Can we hear in it any flicker of the original sacral force of *eusebia*? Derived from an Old French word for "pity", the word "piety" came over into English c. 1540 as a term for religious devotion or "moral vertue" (OED). In modern usage it seems to me to lack the depth and dread of the Greek word – perhaps English has lost touch with true religiosity. Our pieties are more a matter of protocol than dread. And where *eusebia* always implies ritual action, "piety" represents a mood rather than a pressure to act. Nonetheless, there we are. I could not find, I do not know, a different or a better translation. The actor who speaks line 943 on stage will evoke the permanent elsewhere of our longing for the love of gods by drawing it up from her own voice and being.

Second example.

The ancient Greeks did not like mixture. (Forgive this blatant generalization – translator's notes are, by their brevity, blatant). Dirt, in the ancient definition, is matter out of place. The poached egg on your plate at breakfast is not dirt, the poached egg on the floor of the British Museum is. Dirt is matter that has crossed a boundary it ought not to have crossed; dirt confounds categories and mixes up form. Its name in Greek is *miasma*, whose basic sense is "defilement" or "impairment of the integrity of a thing."

Throughout the play Kreon makes clear his preference for pure categories: friend, enemy; patriot, traitor; winner, loser; good, bad; me, them. The final scene of the play forces him to recognize the miscegenation of all these and to see his own boundaries penetrated by everything bad. Recognition is expressed in the language of dirt. As he holds his son's dead body in his arms he asks,

> O filth of death
> who can clean you out
>
> (1284–5)

And a few lines later, standing over the body of his wife:

> now I am perfectly blended with pain
>
> (1311)

It is Aristotle's dictum that a tragic plot is most effective when the recognition and the reversal happen at one blow. Certainly that happens here. But let us probe a little deeper into the effectiveness of Kreon's recognition/reversal. The word he uses at 1311 for "perfectly blended" is a compound of the basic verb "to mix" and the prefix *syn-*, meaning "with." This verb is meant to remind us of all the horrific comminglings that made the house of Oidipous famous, and of which Antigone is a product. But more importantly, it reminds us that Antigone herself was the champion of "withness" from the beginning of the play until her death. Her defiant announcement to Kreon:

> I am someone born to share in love not hatred
>
> (523)

contains two verbs that begin with the same prefix: *synechthein* ("to hate with") and *synphilein* ("to love with"). Withness is Antigone's morality, Antigone's desire, Antigone's disaster. She begins the play yearning to join her brother in the grave:

> one day we'll lie together in the grave he and
> I side by side
>
> (75–6)

And her final lament brings her to a tragic recognition:

> I'm a strange new kind of inbetween thing aren't I
> not at home with the dead nor with the living
>
> (850–1)

Withness – reversed – is nowhere.

Translation cannot convey the complex interactions of this metaphorical system or the inevitability of the catastrophe to which it leads. Antigone and Kreon stand opposed to one another instinctually, in the very morphology of their language, in the very grain of the way they think and speak. Sophoklean tragedy has a quality of tidiness that can be terrifying. He tucks in every stray thread. Or rather he makes it seem that each of these threads was always already woven into the same net. Why did anyone think they could escape?

1 The term "permanent elsewhere" is borrowed from Judith Butler's discussion of Hegel in *Antigone's Claim* (New York, 2000) p. 43.

Characters

ANTIGONE

ISMENE
sister of Antigone

KREON
king of Thebes

HAIMON
son of Kreon and Eurydike

EURYDIKE
wife of Kreon, mother of Haimon

TEIRESIAS
blind prophet of Thebes [led by a boy]

BOY

GUARD

MESSENGER

CHORUS OF OLD THEBAN MEN

Set:

Palace of Kreon at Thebes

ANTIGONE by Sophokles in a new translation by Anne Carson
Anne Carson's new translation opened in Luxembourg, 25 February 2015, and subsequently London, 5 March 2015, at the Barbican Theatre, starring Juliette Binoche under Ivo van Hove's direction.

Produced by the **Barbican** and **Les Théâtres de la Ville de Luxembourg**, in association with **Toneelgroep Amsterdam**
Co-produced by **Théâtre de la Ville–Paris, Ruhrfestspiele Recklinghausen** and **Edinburgh International Festival**

Cast
Antigone **Juliette Binoche**
Guard/Chorus **Obi Abili**
Ismene/Chorus **Kirsty Bushell**
Haimon/Chorus **Samuel Edward-Cook**
Teiresias/Chorus **Finbar Lynch**
Kreon **Patrick O'Kane**
Eurydike/Chorus **Kathryn Pogson**

Creative Team
Director **Ivo van Hove**
Set and Lighting **Jan Versweyveld**
Dramaturg **Peter van Kraaij**
Video **Tal Yarden**
Composition and Sound **Daniel Freitag**
Costumes **An d'Huys**

[enter Antigone and Ismene]

ANTIGONE: we come out of the dark
O Ismene
O one and only sister whose blood intersects with my own in too many ways
ever since we were born from the evils of Oidipous
what bitterness pain disgust disgrace or moral shock
have we been spared
and now this edict
you've heard the edict
or are you unaware
of the evils coming on us

ISMENE: I've heard no news at all
neither sweet nor bitter
that our two brothers are dead by one another's hands
and the Argive army gone from this city
is all I know

ANTIGONE: that's what I thought
that's why I called you out here

ISMENE: what's the matter
you have your thunder look

ANTIGONE: Kreon is resolved
to honour one of our brothers with burial
the other not
Eteokles he has laid in the ground in accordance with justice and law
Polyneikes is to lie unwept and unburied
sweet sorrymeat for the little lusts of the birds
good Kreon draws our attention to this edict
yours and my attention
whoever transgresses it gets death
so what do you say
will you show what you're made of

ISMENE: what could I show
what could I say

what could I do that would make any difference

ANTIGONE: if you join me
if you join my action

ISMENE: at what risk
where is your mind

ANTIGONE: if you help me
help me lift the corpse

ISMENE: you mean bury him
when it's forbidden

ANTIGONE: dear sister, my dead are mine
and yours as well as mine
do what you like but
I will not betray him

ISMENE: Kreon says the act is unlawful

ANTIGONE: Antigone says it's not Kreon's business

ISMENE: O sister, don't cross this line
whoever we are
think, sister –
father's daughter
daughter's brother
sister's mother
mother's son
his mother and his wife were one!
our family is doubled tripled degraded and dirty in every direction
he shattered his own eyeballs so as not to see it
and now our brothers lie slain by one another's hands
so that's it
we two are alone
moreover we're girls
girls cannot force their way against men
I'm sure the dead will forgive me
if I obey those in power
you always push the limit
limits are there for a reason

ANTIGONE: you know what, Ismene?
I wouldn't take your help now if you asked me
yet I will bury him
and this is right to do
though I die for it
one day we'll lie together in the grave he and I side by side
for death is long
death is very long
you go on worrying about the gods of life

ISMENE: I must worry
I'm powerless

ANTIGONE: good excuse
well I'm off
a brother needs burying

ISMENE: I fear for you

ANTIGONE: don't bother

ISMENE: well at least keep this secret

ANTIGONE: oh no, proclaim it to all! I insist!

ISMENE: your heart's so hot O sister

ANTIGONE: the dead are cold
they'll welcome me

ISMENE: you are someone in love with the impossible

ANTIGONE: and when my strength is gone I'll stop

ISMENE: this is utterly wrong

ANTIGONE: don't say that or I'll have to hate you
he will hate you too
just let me go
for I'll not suffer anything so grievous as to rob me of a noble death

ISMENE: go then but know
although you go without your mind
you go as one beloved

[exit Antigone and Ismene]

[enter chorus]

CHORUS:

the glories of the world come sharking in all red and gold
we won the war
salvation struts
the streets of sevengated Thebes
the man from Argos fled
the one who
swung above our land on snowhite screams
the one who

overweened our walls: Polyneikes!
seven spears in his mouth instead of teeth
that one fled
before filling his cheeks with blood
before any fire
the noise of war was stretched along his back
the boaster
fled

Zeus hates a boaster
saw an ocean of them coming at us
raised his hand
they hit the ground
they were
the man from Argos
war
made them all insane

seven gates
and in each gate a man
and in each man a death
at the seventh gate
two brothers
grew
into each other's hearts
as pain

now victory is ours
let there be forgetting
let Thebes shake with joy!

but
here comes Kreon
rowing his new policies into place
what new policies I wonder
and why has he called us here
so formally?

[enter Kreon]

KREON: gentlemen
first let me say
our city is safe again today
although a violent storm passed through
the gods have set us upright
now as to you yourselves
I have sent for you especially
because of your traditional support for Laios
his throne and power
your support for Oidipous
when he restored our city
your support for Oidipous' sons
after Oidipous died
you stood by them you gave solid counsel
well now they're both dead
they fought each other hand to hand
a single day
a double doom
an unholy outcome

I am the throne and power now
(I was the next of kin)

impossible to know the character mentality or judgment of a man
until you see him manage laws and government
it's my view

to steer a city
you need topnotch advisors
and you can't be afraid to say what you think
that's my view (as I say) and always has been
but another thing
and this is important
if a man puts family or friends ahead of fatherland
I count him absolutely *good for nothing*

now as for me –
let Zeus who sees all things take note of this -
to watch ruin advancing upon our citizens and hold my tongue
I could not
to call a man my friend if he were hostile to the land
I could not

sail your city straight and you'll make the right friends
that's my philosophy
those are my laws
here's my edict
concerning Oidipous' sons
for Eteokles
patriot champion hero of our city
our decree is
burial with every kind of holy honour owed to the best of the dead below
for his brother
Polyneikes
who came back from exile meaning to burn us to the ground
to eat our blood
to throw us into slavery
for this man
our decree is
he shall have no grave
no one will bury him
no one will mourn him
no one will utter a cry
leave him out for the birds to peck and the dogs to chew and the eye to be outraged at
evildoers
have no status in my city

this is a place for law-abiding men
whoever is loyal
alive or dead
will have honour from me

CHORUS: if that's what you want to do, Kreon, do it
you have the power
you can use the law as you like
both for the dead and all of us who are living

KREON: but now it's for you to keep watch on all this

CHORUS: oh can't you ask a younger man

KREON: I don't mean watch the grave I've got people doing that already

CHORUS: so what are your orders

KREON: be careful you don't collaborate with anyone disloyal to me

CHORUS: who could be so rash so suicidal

KREON: exactly
but there is such a thing as blind hope
not to mention bribery

[enter Guard]

GUARD:
king
here I am and I admit
I'm not out of breath
I can't say I hurried
in fact I stopped many times on the road and thought to go back
saying to myself
you fool
what are you doing
why are you going
you know you'll suffer
saying to myself
wretch
don't keep stopping
if Kreon finds out all this from somebody else you're finished

back and forth I argued with me
it was a long trip on a slow road
finally I decided
I'd come and tell what I have to tell
how bad can it be

KREON: so what's the problem

GUARD: first
let me say first
I didn't do it
I don't know who did it
I shouldn't pay the price for this

KREON: stop hedging
give me your news

GUARD: it's terrible news
is why I hesitate

KREON: *you goat's anus,* talk

GUARD: okay
the corpse someone buried it
someone threw dust on it someone did all the required holy stuff

KREON: what are you saying
what man would have dared

GUARD:
I have no idea
was the ground hard and dry yes
was there any mark or scratch or so much as a wagon rut no
whoever did that he left no clue
we were all in shock
you can't see the body any more
there's no real burial mound just light dust over it
but enough to clear the curse
no sign of animals or dogs or depredation
so then
we fell to shouting
guard against guard

we fell to blows
each of us was the guilty one
no one for sure
who could be sure
we were ready for the red hot iron each of us swearing to gods
I didn't do it I know nothing getting nowhere
then someone said *better tell Kreon*
and we stood paralyzed
staring at the ground
we knew he was right it couldn't be hushed up
so lucky me
we all drew lots and here I am
I don't want to see you you don't want to see me but here I am

CHORUS: you know, king
it's been my feeling for a long time now
that gods are mixed up in this somehow

KREON: don't say another word
don't be that stupid
gods mixed up in this
you demented old men
you think *the gods* buried him for his good intentions
you think *the gods* gave him a prize for citizenship
despite the fact he came to burn their temples down
to desecrate their laws
you think the gods find gangsters like that *honourable*
well here's a simple truth
I'll say it one time
you're wrong
gods didn't do this but there are men who would try
men who don't like me
men who murmur and fret and chafe under my government
men who might well lead a guard or a watchman astray with a bit of a bribe
in fact
now that I think of it
that's exactly what happened
money's a nasty invention isn't it
it ruins cities and men

turns good minds to bad
and has discovered every crime and misdemeanour known to human beings

whoever took a bribe to do this deed will pay the price
now *you [to Guard]* listen
I swear by Zeus himself – yes I still honour Zeus –
if you don't find and bring to me the guilty man
I'll make you beg for death
I'll have you hanging by your thumbs till you confess
you greedy pissant little amateur terrorist

GUARD: can I say something or should I just go

KREON: you're treading a very thin line

GUARD: would you say it's your ears or your mind that finds me annoying

KREON: do you really want to test my mood like this

GUARD: because I mean if it's the ears
blame me
but if it's the mind
blame the man who did the deed

KREON: you were born already babbling weren't you

GUARD: yes but I wasn't born to do this deed

KREON: yet you did
they bribed you
they bought your soul

GUARD: no
it's a lie
a deadly awful lie

KREON: of course you would say that
well, produce the perpetrator
or you're guilty

[exit Kreon]

GUARD: sure we'll find the guy
but if we don't

let's say he gets lucky
there's no way you'll see me back here again
right now I'll just say thank gods I'm still alive

[exit Guard]

CHORUS:

many things strange
terrible
clever
wondrous
monstrous
marvellous
dreadful
awful
and
weird
there are in the world
but none more
strange
terrible
clever
uncanny
wondrous
monstrous
marvellous
dreadful
awful
and
weird
than Man
he sails across the sea in blasting winter
he ploughs the inexhaustible earth year after year

the race of birds
the tribes of beasts
the underwater creatures all
he drives into his net
this clever man
he masters animals that roam the hills

and puts wild horses to the yoke or mountain bulls

he uses thought and language and the tempering of these
he knows to shelter from the frost and rain
and how to shun disease
he answers
every question put to him
every question put to him
                    but one
                    to Death he has no answer
                    from Death he finds no exit

oh yes he is ingenious
an ingenuity
leading now to good and now to bad
but
the man who honours the laws of the land
the man who keeps the justice of gods
walks high in his high city
cityless
he becomes
if he takes it upon himself
to do wrong
I would not have that person at my hearth
nor share in his opinions

[enter Guard with Antigone]

is there something supernatural going on here
I think there is
I fear there is
here comes Antigone I can't deny it
O you poor awful child of poor awful Oidipous
why do they drag you like a criminal
surely it wasn't you defied the king's law

GUARD: this is the one she did it she did the deed
we caught her burying him
where's Kreon

CHORUS: here's Kreon

perfect timing

[enter Kreon]

KREON: here's Kreon
perfect for what

GUARD: well, king, miracles do happen
I swore I wouldn't come back
but I did
it's the last thing I expected
but here I am
and pretty pleased
because I caught her she's the one I caught her she did it she was fiddling with the grave
no casting lots this time
just my own unique and personal good luck
so there you have it
she's the one you want
take her
try her
convict her
I'm off the hook

KREON: fiddling what do you mean fiddling
explain how you caught her

GUARD: she was burying him
that's all I know

KREON: are you absolutely sure of what you're saying

GUARD: the corpse
the illegal
I saw her burying him
what more do you want

KREON: burying him how when where did you see her how did you catch her
details I want details

GUARD: details okay
you threatened me I went back wiped off all the dust left that body bare

we sat up on the hill was it hot yes
was there putrefaction and vermiculation yes
was there noonsunstink yes
did I doze off no I did not
we were keeping each other awake with jibes and banter and time oh time
went by time went by and the huge white sun
in the centre of the sky
and
all of a sudden
a storm blew up a
pillar of dust all the way to the sky a wind
tore the hair off the trees and all the place was vibrating
we shut our eyes was it godsent thing? I sneaked a look there
she was
the child
making that weird little bird sound you know
how they cry when they see the nest empty
so she cried seeing the body bare
so she cried and called down curses
on whoever did the deed
then she pours dust onto the body with both hands
she pours water onto the body with both hands
three libations to crown the corpse
and we rush out and take her
she seems unsurprised
she denies nothing
it made me sad
but also happy
sad for her happy for me
self-preservation is my natural philosophy

KREON *[to Antigone]*: and you with your head down you're the one
you did this deed you do not deny it

ANTIGONE: I did the deed I do not deny it

KREON *[to Guard]*: go
you're a lucky man today

[exit Guard]

KREON *[to Antigone]*: answer me this and no long speeches
you knew this deed to be forbidden by decree

ANTIGONE: of course I did

KREON. and yet you dared to disobey the law

ANTIGONE: well if you call that *law*

KREON: I do

ANTIGONE: Zeus does not
Justice does not
what they call *law* did not begin today or yesterday
when they say *law* they do not mean a statute of today or yesterday
they mean the unwritten unfaltering unshakable ordinances of the gods
that no human being can ever outrun
these laws live forever
no one knows how they were born
you thought I would transgress them
for fear of some mere mortal man's decree?
no
of course I will die
Kreon or no Kreon
and death is *fine*
death has no pain
to leave my mother's son lying out there unburied that would be pain
you say this is folly
I say who knows folly better than a fool

CHORUS: got a soul as raw as her father doesn't she
no sense of compromise

KREON: here's something to ponder
say we have a piece of iron baked in the fire till it's super hard
I can show you how to smash it
I've seen high-spirited horses broken to a tiny tiny bit
slaves shouldn't think big
this girl knew her act was criminal
when she broke the law that I decreed
criminal insulting and wrong the first time
wrong all the more the second time

and she *boasts* of it she *laughs*
surely *I* am not a man here
she is the man
if she wins this trick and walks away
I don't care if she is my sister's child
or someone closer to me than my whole family
I don't care if she's protected by Zeus
she won't evade doom
neither she nor her sister
oh I know they're in it together
why don't you call that one out here too
I saw her in the house just now getting hysterical
so the criminal mind betrays itself, does it not
I hate secrets
I hate people who try to glamorize a crime once they're caught

ANTIGONE: what do you desire other than my death

KREON: nothing whatsoever

ANTIGONE: then can we get this over with
I take no pleasure in your words
nor you in mine
and yet what greater glory could I win
than to lay my own brother in his grave
these people here would all agree with me
if they weren't terrified
one-man rule has its advantages doesn't it

KREON: you're the only person in Thebes who sees things this way

ANTIGONE: no actually they all do
but you've nailed their tongues to the floor

KREON: you're not ashamed

ANTIGONE: no shame in honouring one's kin

KREON: wasn't the other brother your kin too

ANTIGONE: same mother same father

KREON: yet you don't mind disgracing him

ANTIGONE: he will not call it disgrace

KREON: of course he will you're honouring his enemy

ANTIGONE: it was no slave that died it was his brother

KREON: the one a criminal the other a defender of our land

ANTIGONE: Death needs to have Death's laws obeyed

KREON: same law for good and evil patriot and traitor

ANTIGONE: who knows how these definitions work down there

KREON: enemy is always enemy alive or dead

ANTIGONE: I am someone born to share in love not hatred

KREON: then go down below
and lavish your love on the dead
I will *not* be bested by a woman

[enter Ismene]

CHORUS: here's Ismene she seems to be
weeping flushed and troubled

KREON: you
you've been snaking around my house
sucking me dry
planning ruin and subversion the two of you
come clean now tell me
you joined her in this burial did you not
or will you claim ignorance

ISMENE: I did the deed I share the blame
just ask her

ANTIGONE: no! justice forbids this
you did nothing you shared nothing

ISMENE: I'm not ashamed to help you in your trouble

ANTIGONE: who did the deed?
the actual deed

ask Hades
ask the dead below
I don't like this sudden sympathy of yours it's all words

ISMENE: please, sister, do not exclude me from the right
to die with you and share our brother's requiem

ANTIGONE: leave my death alone
you did not lay a hand on this
you cannot make it yours
for me to die is altogether adequate

ISMENE: I'll be so lonely

ANTIGONE: apply to Kreon
he's your main concern anyway

ISMENE: why are you so nasty
how does it help you

ANTIGONE: you're right it doesn't help
I simply pain myself when I mock you

ISMENE: but can I not help you
somehow

ANTIGONE: save yourself
I do not grudge you this

ISMENE: oh no oh no
am I to miss out on your destiny

ANTIGONE: you chose life I chose death

ISMENE: but I told you and told you and told you not to

ANTIGONE: yes you did and that made sense for you
but this makes sense for me

ISEMENE: yet look we two are equally at fault

ANTIGONE: take heart and live, Ismene
my soul died long ago
so it might serve the dead

KREON: look at them now they're crazy both of them
this one's been that way since she was born

ISMENE: it's true, king
bad conditions make people lose their minds

KREON: as you did
when you chose to side with a criminal

ISMENE: how could I go on in life without her

KREON: don't mention her
she is no more

ISMENE: and will you execute your own son's bride

KREON: oh he'll find other ruts to plough

ISMENE: he won't find anyone else like her

KREON: to think of that marriage makes me sick

ISMENE: dearest Haimon, how your father disregards you

KREON: enough talk of beds it's disgusting

ISMENE: you really will take her away from him

KREON: Death will do the taking

ISMENE: so it's settled then
Antigone dies

KREON: we both know that
don't waste my time

[to Guard] take them inside
and tie them up
no more free-running women
even the boldest of them will take to their heels
if they see Death nearby

[exit Antigone, Ismene]

CHORUS:

blessed be they whose lives do not taste of evil

but if some god shakes your house
ruin arrives
ruin does not leave
it comes tolling over the generations
it comes rolling the black night silt up from the ocean floor
and all your thrashed coasts groan

archives of grief I see falling upon this house
death on birth birth on death there is no end to it
some god is piling them on
one last root was reaching up for light in the house of Oidipous
but the hacksaw of death
is mowing it down

Zeus you win you always win
the whole oxygen of power
belongs to you
sleep cannot seize it
time does not tire it
your Mt Olympos glows like one white stone upon this law
nothing vast enters the lives of mortals
without ruin

but of course there is hope look here comes hope
wandering in
to tickle your feet
then you notice the soles are on fire
a wise word
if you find you're confusing evil with good
some god is heading you down the high road to ruin
watch out

oh here's Haimon
your youngest son
does he come
in pain and rage
cheated of his future bride

[enter Haimon]

KREON: you've heard the verdict on your future bride

so are you in a rage against your father, child
or are we still friends

HAIMON: father, I'm yours
I trust your judgment
no marriage could outweigh this

KREON: good attitude, son
good heart in your chest
a father needs a son to back him up
this is why men beget sons
to harm their enemies and honour their friends
some children are useless
some are just trouble
and who would disagree
this makes people *laugh at the father*
a fact of life I'll say to you now I'll say it one time
when you lay yourself under a pleasure female
the pleasure goes cold soon enough
she's an open wound in your house and your life
she's an enemy
spit her out
let her go seduce some boy in hell
you know she disobeyed me publicly and flagrantly
alone out of all the city
I will not be made a liar
I'll put her to death
let her call on Zeus and blood and kinship who cares
should I nourish disorder within my own family?
how then control those outside it?
a man who runs his household right
can run a government
he's staunch in war loyal in action
on the other hand someone who flouts the laws
or thinks to give instruction to the rulers
him I do not praise
if the city sets up a man to rule it I say
that man *must* be obeyed
in small things and just things and the opposite of these

anarchy! what greater evil
anarchy is what ruins citics and houses and battle plans
obedience saves lives
obedience must be defended
and *never never never* let ourselves be bested by a woman

CHORUS: well that was all pretty plausible
or so it seemed to me

HAIMON: father, the gods grow minds in men
as the most precious equipment they have
yet I could not would not do not know how to
say you are wrong
who knows it might all turn out fine
but surely my job is to keep a close watch
on everything people do or say or want to complain about
why your dread eye your displeasure what people say, well
you wouldn't want to hear the kind of things they say
but I can listen from the shadows
this girl
through the town
there is grief
they call her wonderful
most glorious of deeds most terrible of deaths (they say) she only chose
to keep her brother's body from rawflesh-eating dogs
to keep it from the birds this sort of talk
I don't know
from the shadows
nothing is more precious to me than your happiness, father
for a son to be proud of his father
a father proud of his son
what could be better
but please don't be so absolutely singleminded
whoever imagines he alone is the one
who knows how to think or speak or feel
that man is an empty page
there's nothing shameful in being a person able to learn
flexible
not too rigid

you've seen trees bend in a storm
that's how they save their branches
the stubborn ones get ripped out by the roots
in sailing too
if you haul your sheets taut you'll capsize the boat
let go your anger, father
give a bit
I'm young yes
but I'm pretty sure of this
no single human being has perfect knowledge
most of us would be wise now and then to take advice

CHORUS: well, king, he hit the nail on the head a few times there
you could learn something from him
and you [*to Haimon*] from him

KREON: me at my age go to school and get wisdom from this stripling

HAIMON: you would learn nothing unjust

KREON: nothing unjust to honour anarchy

HAIMON: I do not honour anarchy

KREON: is the girl not tainted with that malady

HAIMON: the whole city of Thebes says otherwise

KREON: shall Thebes prescribe to me how I should rule

HAIMON: listen to yourself you sound like a boy dictator

KREON: whom else should the government depend on

HAIMON: no city belongs to a single man

KREON: surely a city belongs to its ruler

HAIMON: why not find a desert and rule all alone

KREON [*to the chorus*]: this fellow it seems is the woman's toy

HAIMON: if *you* are the woman
it's you I care for

KREON: O shameless thou utter miscreant
to prosecute thine own father

HAIMON: yes for I see you doing wrong

KREON: wrong to respect mine own prerogatives

HAIMON: you don't respect you trample on the prerogatives of the gods

KREON: O polluted O dastard nature O subject to a woman

HAIMON: but not subject to injustice

KREON: all thy words plead for her

HAIMON: and for you and for me and the gods below

KREON: thou canst never marry her this side the grave

HAIMON: then she'll die and take another with her

KREON: doth thy boldness push thee even to threats

HAIMON: threats what threats I merely point out your judgment is bad

KREON: thou shalt rue the day of thy witless teaching

HAIMON: if you weren't my father I'd say you'd lost your mind

KREON: thou woman's chattel seek not to tickle me

HAIMON: you talk and talk and never listen

KREON: sayest thou so well now well now I say
thou shalt revile me to thy cost
fetch out the loathéd thing
let her die hard against her bridegroom now this very instant before his eyes

HAIMON: never no never
if I am near she will not die
and you'll not see my face again, ever
rage on, madman

[exit Haimon]

CHORUS: well he's gone
in anger and pain

a young man like that
who knows what he'll do

KREON: let him go
Big Man
I have executions to perform
two of them

CHORUS: you mean to kill both girls

KREON: no you're right
just the meddlesome one

CHORUS: how will you do it

KREON: I'll find her a desert
in the neighbourhood
I'll bury her alive
with a bit of food
just enough to avoid the pollution, a sort of
sacred technicality
no doubt if she prays hard
the gods of death will save her life
or else she'll learn
she picked the wrong gods

[exit Kreon]

CHORUS:

Eros, no one can fight you
Eros, you clamp down on every living thing
on a girl's cheek on oceans on wild fields
not even an immortal can evade you
certainly not a creature of the day
why
they go mad

you change the levels of a person's mind
this Haimon-crisis is all your doing
you shook his blood
you glow on girls' eyelids
what do you care about the laws of the land

Aphrodite, you play with us you
play
deeply

[enter Antigone]

CHORUS: well, I'm having my own doubts about the laws of the land
and I no longer can restrain a stream of tears
when I see Antigone here passing
to the room where we all
go in the end

ANTIGONE: look at me
people
I go my last road
I see my last light
look
Death who gathers all of us into his old bent arms in the end
is gathering me
but I am still alive
no wedding
no wedding song
no wedding chamber
yet I shall lie as a bride in the bed of the river of Death
while I am still alive

CHORUS: oh yes but won't you win glory
won't you be praised
it's not as if you're dying of disease or war
you chose to live autonomous
and so you die
the only one of mortals to go down to Death alive

ANTIGONE: what about Niobe I've heard that she
has a living death like me
inside a piece of rock
for a mountain grows over her like ivy
and the rain and snow run down her face
she is laid to bed (like me) by some divinity

CHORUS: but Niobe was a god

born of gods
we are mortal
born of mortals
and yet
what a great thing
to share your story with divinity
while you live and while you die

ANTIGONE: are you mockers of me
you grabbing old men
are you laughers at me
though I'm not yet gone
O springs of the rivers of Thebes
O reaches of the plains of Thebes
bear me witness
no one sheds a tear for me
as I go to my strange new grave
no one knows what kind of laws they are that sentence me
nor what kind of tomb it is I go to
I'm a strange new kind of inbetween thing aren't I
not at home with the dead nor with the living

CHORUS: you're too extreme
you reckless girl
you can't simply kick justice out of the way
and given your father's history I'd say
you're paying off his debts

ANTIGONE: ah there you touch
the deepest bitterest place in me
pity for my father
all that plowing in the dark
and the brilliant house of Labdakos gone down in it
father mother mother son it all went wrong
from what kind of badness was I born
accursed
unwed
alien foreign and strange
I am nowhere at home on this earth
I go to them now

a final family reunion
O my brother how you despoil me by your death

CHORUS: well
piety is nice but authority is authority
you have in you a kind of absolute exclusive self-regarding rage
it has destroyed you

ANTIGONE: unwept
unwed
unloved
I go
the road is there before me
this light of day is not for my eyes anymore
who will lament me
no one will lament me

[enter Kreon]

KREON: if people could lament their own deaths right up until they died
no one would ever stop
[to Guard] take her away take her quickly
I have told you how to prison her in rock
and leave her there to die or live as she sees fit
we are clean of this girl
her privileges on earth are here revoked

ANTIGONE: O tomb
O bridal chamber
O house in the ground forever
I go to you
I go to meet my people
now numbered among the dead
father
mother
brother
I am the last and worst of you
open your arms to me, dear ones
I buried you all
even you, Polyneikes
I lifted and washed you and made you lovely

and this is my reward
people ask
would I have done it for a husband or a child
my answer is no I would not
people ask
what law requires this
I say
a husband or a child can be replaced
but who can grow me a new brother
this is the law I honoured before everything
and Kreon calls it criminal
he says I like to fondle strange and reckless things
oh beloved brother
he is taking me away
I never had a bridal bed I never had a bridal song
I never had the love of children
I'm alone on my insides
and I go down to death though I am still alive
what kind of justice is this
why look to gods
why hope for allies
they call my piety impiety
I say fine, if the gods do really approve of this
I'll recognize my error soon enough
but if these men here are the criminals
may they suffer exactly what they are doing to me

CHORUS: your soul is blowing apart

KREON: get a move on

ANTIGONE: next word
is death

KREON: DEATH
you have no way out

ANTIGONE: O Thebes
O gods
O look
I go

you valid men of Thebes
I'm the last one left in a line of kings
look at what is happening to me
and look at the men who are doing it
I was caught
in an act
of perfect
piety

[exit Antigone]

CHORUS:
I'll give you three examples
of people who lost access to the light
first the girl called Danaë
they walled her up in a room and put a yoke on her
yet she was precious (you know the story)
economist of Zeus' gold
in a sexual shower
what does this tell us?
the power of fate (whatever that is) is
a strange
terrible
clever
uncanny
wondrous
monstrous
marvellous
dreadful
awful
weird
power

example two Lykourgos
an angry child who grew up to be an angry king
and for venting his anger on Dionysos
he was confined in a room of rock
where he came to know the god
intimately
and the strange mad flower of his mind

dripped in the dark

third example the woman
who blinded her sons with a shuttle cock
and the blood ran down her hands
ruin ran down
now it's true she was born of Boreas
and could outrace the wind
but fate came down hard on her too in the end
fate (whatever it is, some sort of god)
comes down on
everyone
in the end

[enter Teiresias led by a boy]

TEIRESIAS [to the chorus]: hail, you kings of Thebes
we've come
two people seeing as one
it is the blind man's way

KREON: what's up Teiresias

TEIRESIAS *[to Kreon]*: I'll tell you
and you must do what the seer says

KREON: I've followed your advice before

TEIRESIAS: and so you kept the city going straight

KREON: indeed I owe you much

TEIRESIAS: you're standing on a razor's edge

KREON: what
why
I feel suddenly cold

TEIRESIAS: listen then, listen and learn
I was sitting in the place I always sit
a sanctuary for every kind of bird
I'm listening to their voices
and it all sounds *wrong*

wild and weird like monsters
tearing at each other with their talons
thrashing at each other with their wings
fear comes into me
I turn to the altar
but the fires won't light
the embers sputter
the fat slides off the bones
the boy described it all to me
he is my guide as I am guide for others
now you know, Kreon
the failing of the signs is in itself a sign
and surely
these signs failed
and surely
the cause is you
you bring this sickness on the city
you gave that body to the birds and dogs so that
our hearths and altars are defiled
of course the gods have turned away from us
of course the birds are shrieking unintelligible things
their mouths are gorged with guts and blood
my child, take heed
to err is human
but to persist in error is imprudent unlucky and just stupid
yield, Kreon
that pile of rot that was the son of Oidipous
the boy is dead stop killing him

I mean you well
I give you good advice
take it

KREON: you're a nice old man but
all you seers are just mediocre marksmen
firing arrows at a man like me
I've been the victim of your "art of prophecy" before
been bought and sold and trafficked by your tribe
so fine

run your scam
take your profit
you will not lay that body in the grave
not even if the very eagles of Zeus decide to rip its flesh and carry
bits of it up to the throne of god
let me repeat
you will not lay that body in the grave
no I don't fear pollution
human beings cannot pollute the gods
I know this for a fact
but human beings are susceptible
aren't they, dear old Teiresias
to the profit-motive
especially the clever ones

TEIRESIAS: alas
isn't anyone listening
doesn't anyone get it

KREON: get what

TEIRESIAS: good judgment good judgment
nothing is more important

KREON: well yes, and bad judgment can do great harm

TEIRESIAS: you are rotten with it, Kreon, you are full of this disease

KREON: I'm in no mood to trade sarcasms with a seer

TEIRESIAS: and yet your denounce my profession

KREON: your profession! that bunch of entrepreneurs

TEIRESIAS: while you tyrants grab anything you want without shame

KREON: don't you realize you're talking to your king

TEIRESIAS: oh I do
who put you in this kingship
who helped you save the city

KREON: prophet or not, you're dangerously fond of injustice

TEIRESIAS: you will provoke me to say things I keep in the dark of my heart

KREON: oh say them
forget profit

TEIRESIAS: do you really think I've been profiting up to now

KREON: just recognize you cannot buy my mind

TEIRESIAS: well then recognize this, Kreon
not many revolutions of the sun from this day
you shall have paid the price
a corpse for a corpse
the life of your only begotten child
for you've housed a living soul beneath the ground below
and held a dead man here
without his grave or rights
it is so wrong
it is so wrong
the dead do not belong to you
nor to the gods above
you violate these rules
there are avengers lying in wait for you now, watch out
watch out I say and think again
whether I am someone who's been paid to say this

not long now
there will be wailing of men and wailing of women
there will be tumult of cities and hatred against you
dogs and birds and body parts and stench *you can't do that*
these are the arrows I loose against you
like an archer, yes
because you grieve me
because I'm angry
and my arrows fly true
you will not escape their heat

[to the boy] take me home
he can vent his rage on younger men
and find a gentler tongue
a better attitude

[exit Teiresias with boy]

CHORUS: that was harsh but
I've been around a long time and I have to say
historically
his prophecies are never false

KREON: I know
I'm shaking
on the one hand to give in now would be terrible
equally terrible of course to stand fast and be ruined

CHORUS: take advice

KREON: tell me

CHORUS: set the girl free bury the boy

KREON: you really mean this I should just give in

CHORUS: quick quick quick
catastrophe can outrun fools

KREON: it's hard
it's hard but yes I must

CHORUS: quick quick quick
go yourself go *now*

KREON: I go
[to servants] take your axes, one and all
make for the high ground over there
I've changed my mind about this girl
it was I imprisoned her and I shall set her free
I now suspect we have to live our lives
right to the end
in accordance with the old established laws

[exit Kreon]

CHORUS:
O
god of a thousand names
you who are there

begotten of thunder
moving in mystery
master of Thebes where the dragon seed fell
visible in fire
going where rivers go
green in the vine shadow
you who are there
hear our cry
make us well

O
Bakkhos
purify us
set the city right
you who organize the firebreathing stars to dance
and supervise the voices in the night
manager of madness
you who are there
show yourself
hear our cry
grant us light

[enter Messenger]

MESSENGER: citizens
there is no stanza of human life that
I would praise or blame
luck lifts a person up or knocks a person down
at any given moment
fortunate unfortunate
no seer can see what's next
Kreon (I once thought) was an enviable man
for he saved this land of Kadmos from its enemies
he got his hands on monarchy
he sailed it straight and furrows of children flourished around him
now all that's gone
when joy betrays you
I do not count your life alive
a corpse is more alive
be as rich as you like

be a despot absolute
if your happiness goes
I wouldn't buy you for a shadow of smoke

CHORUS: you're the Messenger
what's your message

MESSENGER: they're dead

CHORUS: who's dead

MESSENGER: Haimon's dead

CHORUS: by whose hand

MESSENGER: a hand very like his own
for rage at his father

CHORUS: okay Teiresias, you won that round

MESSENGER: game's not over

CHORUS: you're right
here's Eurydike wife of Kreon
what's she up to

[enter Eurydike]

EURYDIKE: O people
did I overhear something
I was just going out
I was just at the door
I was going to offer prayers to Athena
just opening the door and I thought I heard something
a voice like sorrow
and I fell back I fainted I was struck with fear
whatever the news is
do tell me
sorrow and I are not strangers

MESSENGER: O beloved queen
I was there I will speak
I'll leave nothing out
why soften the tale and be called a liar later

I went with your husband as guide
to the edge of the plain
where it lay
the dogtorn parts
the parts of him
Polyneikes
we prayed the gods to hold back their anger
we washed him and burned him
on freshcut branches
we piled high a mound and we left
to go to the tomb of the girl
the bride of Death
and we're still a ways off
when we hear a scream
from that unholy place
someone comes running but Kreon won't stop
the scream is all around us now
he quickens and lets out a cry to pierce your heart
oh no oh no (he says)
am I the prophet now
could there be a road darker than this road I'm on
is it my own son crying out
go quicker, you people, drag the rocks back and go in
do the gods deceive me
or is that Haimon's voice I hear
poor hopeless king
so we do what he says
and against the back wall
we see her hung by the neck on a strand of silk
the boy flings himself on her body wailing
Kreon sees him runs in with a cry
O my dear darling what have you done
are you mad are you lost O child come away
come out I beg you
then the boy
with eyes like murder
spat in his father's face
he said not a word but drew his sword and lunged
Kreon ran out the boy missed

then in a black rage at himself he
tensed his body for the sword and drove it all the way up to the lung
poor boy was still alive
he folded himself around the girl
and breathed a thread of red red blood onto her white white cheek
so he lay
a corpse on a corpse
and his bridal consummation
was in the house of Death

what does this teach us?
bad judgment
bad judgment
is the worst thing in the world a man can have

[exit Eurydike]

CHORUS: what do you make of that
she left without a word

MESSENGER: I too am surprised
but I nourish the hope
that she felt it unsuitable to grieve in public
and went inside to set the women wailing
for the sorrow of the house
she's a sensitive person

CHORUS: maybe so
maybe so
but it's a very heavy silence
I don't like a heavy silence

MESSENGER: I'll go in and see
you're right
it's too heavy a silence

[exit Messenger]

CHORUS: here comes Kreon
dragging his
dragging his
dragging his what

no one else did this
he did this

[enter Kreon with body of Haimon]

KREON: here is what I did
it was my hard killing mind
it was my deadly goings wrong O look
the killers and the killed are all one family
O my child too soon dead O
this sacrilege that I called public policy
my child this child alas the child
murdered
by my folly

CHORUS: you're late
to learn
what's right
aren't you

KREON: late to learn O yes I am
late too late O then O then
some god slammed down on me with all his weight
some god shook me out in savage directions
alas for the joy of my life that I've trampled underfoot
alas for us all going dark

[enter Messenger]

MESSENGER: O king
you have evils in hand
you have evils in store
soon you will see
grief in the house

KREON: what now
what worse

MESSENGER: your wife is dead
the mother of this one
her wounds are recent

KREON: O filth of Death
who can clean you out
O piling up of Death
who can reckon you
you take a man already broken
and grind him to dust
come tell me your news, messenger
the woman the blood the boy

MESSENGER: see for yourself
she is here

KREON: ah
so she is
so they are
my ruin now complete
my son in my arms
my wife laid out before me
O beloveds
you were his mother
you were her son
O beloveds

MESSENGER: before the end
before undoing her eyes to the dark
she called out one last time on this boy
and she cursed you
assassin of your own child she said

KREON: O yes O yes
of course she did
the horror of it
crawls all over me
will someone strike me dead please
now I am utterly blended with pain

MESSENGER: she blamed you
for all of it

KREON: and then what

MESSENGER: stabbed herself in the liver

KREON: O yes O dear yes
no one else is to blame
I killed you I killed you, O dear one, I did
someone, take Kreon away
he no more exists than someone who does not exist

CHORUS: best to be brief
when evil is all around your feet

KREON: let it come let it come
let my end come
I cannot bear to look upon another day of life

CHORUS: that's the future this is the present
you deal with the present

KREON: to die is my only prayer

CHORUS: then don't pray at all
you don't get to run this

KREON: take Kreon away please take Kreon away
I murdered you both O my beloveds
never intending to
where can I look
where can I turn
everything I touch goes wrong
a fate no one could bear has plunged
down on me

CHORUS: the first rule of a happy life: wisdom
second rule: don't work against the gods
you big men with your big words
pay a big price for that
but in the end
you learn wisdom too
even you